COSTA RICA

Major World Nations
COSTA RICA

Tricia Haynes

CHELSEA HOUSE PUBLISHERS
Philadelphia

306.3493

Chelsea House Publishers

Copyright © 1999 by Chelsea House Publishers,
a division of Main Line Book Co.
All rights reserved.
Printed in Hong Kong

First Printing.

1 3 5 7 9 8 6 4 2

Library of Congress Cataloging-in-Publication Data

Haynes, Tricia.
Costa Rica / Tricia Haynes.
p. cm. — (Major world nations)
Includes index.
Summary: Discusses the history, geography, climate, economy, and people of the Central American nation of Costa Rica.
ISBN 0-7910-4973-6
1. Costa Rica—Juvenile literature. [1. Costa Rica.] I. Title.
II. Series.
F1543.2.H39 1998
972.86—dc21   98-6400
CIP
AC

ACKNOWLEDGEMENTS

The author and publishers are grateful to the following organizations and individuals for permission to reproduce copyright illustrations in this book:
Michael Cannon; The Mansell Collection Ltd.; Carlos Reyes/Andes Press Agency; Peter Ryley; Photothèque Vautier-de Nanxe; Associated Press.

CONTENTS

Map		6
Facts at a Glance		7
History at a Glance		9
Chapter 1	The Rich Coast	13
Chapter 2	Past and Present	24
Chapter 3	The Stable Republic	34
Chapter 4	Living in Costa Rica	43
Chapter 5	Earning a Living	54
Chapter 6	San José: The Quiet Capital	62
Chapter 7	The Port Cities: Puntarenas and Puerto Limón	74
Chapter 8	Guanacaste: Cowboy Country	84
Chapter 9	Costa Rica in the World Today	92
Glossary		99
Index		101

FACTS AT A GLANCE

Land and People

Official Name Republic of Costa Rica (*Republica de Costa Rica*)

Location Costa Rica is located in Central America bordered to the north by Nicaragua, to the northeast by the Caribbean Sea, to the southeast by Panama, and to the west and southwest by the Pacific Ocean

Area 19,730 square miles (51,100 square kilometer)

Climate Subtropical

Capital San José

Other Cities Limón, Alajuela, San Isidor de El General, Desamparados

Population 3.5 million

Population Density 70 persons per square kilometer

Major Rivers San Juan, Rio Grande, Reventazon

Mountains Cordillera de Guanacaste, Cordillera Central, Cordillera de Talamanca

Official Languages	Spanish, English, German
Religions	Roman Catholic (80 percent), Protestants (15 percent), Methodists, Baptists, Quakers, Mormons
Literacy Rate	90 percent

Economy

Natural Resources	Petroleum, natural gas, bauxite, manganese
Agricultural Products	Sugarcane, bananas, pineapples, rice, oranges, coffee, cassava, plantains, palm oil, potatoes, beef
Industries	Forestry, fishing, mining, manufacturing, tourism
Major Imports	Raw materials, nondurable and durable consumer goods, capital goods for industry
Major Exports	Bananas, coffee, textiles, clothing, footwear, fish, shrimp, ornamental plants, leaves and flowers
Currency	Costa Rican *colón*

Government

Form of Government	Democracy
Government Bodies	Legislative Assembly
Formal Head of State	President
Voting Rights	All citizens over the age of 18 can vote

HISTORY AT A GLANCE

1000 B.C. First known artifacts of the Diquis, the most important of the several dozen Indian tribes of Costa Rica.

500 A.D.-800 A.D. The Diquis come into contact with other peoples of the Americas who influence their artistic styles.

1502 Christopher Columbus, during his fourth voyage, lands on coast of present-day Costa Rica. Columbus gives the coastal area of Honduras, Costa Rica, and Panama the name "Veragua."

1506 Diego de Nicuesa is sent by Spain to occupy the territory. He is shipwrecked, then attacked by hostile natives. The expedition is abandoned.

1521-1522 The expedition of Gil Gonzalez comes up Costa Rica's Pacific coast from Panama.

1540 Costa Rica formally organized as a Spanish province.

1560 The conquistadors Juan de Cavallon and Juan Vasquez de Coronado leave the Pacific coast and penetrate to the Valle Central, the site of the present capital San José.

1562	Juan Vasquez de Coronado becomes governor, and soon establishes a capital at Cartago, in the Valle Central.
1579	Sir Francis Drake lands on the Caribbean coast. The coast becomes a frequent stopping place for English pirates.
1611-1660	Smallpox, influenza, measles and other diseases brought in by Spanish settlers devastate native population. Indians decline from 80,000 to less than a hundred.
1635	Virgin Mary is said to have appeared to a peasant girl on August 2, taking the form of a dark stone doll, "La Negrita," in a location which is now part of Cartago. The doll is still preserved at a basilica built on the spot and Nuestra Senora de los Angeles has become the patron saint of Costa Rica.
1706	Settlers found a second city, modern-day Heredía.
1737	The town of Boca del Monte founded in the Valle Central, later to be known as San José.
1780	A British expedition under the young Horatio Nelson captures a fort on Costa Rican territory. The expedition is eventually defeated by disease, bad weather and difficult terrain.
1808	Coffee plants brought to Costa Rica from Jamaica.
1808-1810	Revolts against Spanish rule break out in Latin America. Simon Bolivar of Venezuela emerges as the principal leader of the independence forces. Costa Rica is still a colonial backwater, and the revolts have little impact there.

1823	Spanish forces defeated throughout South America. United Provinces of Central America formed on July 1, including Guatemala, El Salvador, Honduras, Nicaragua, and Costa Rica.
1824	Guanacaste province, a cattle-raising area, votes to join Costa Rica after also being claimed by Nicaragua. This makes Costa Rica a substantially bigger country.
1838	United Provinces breaks up into separate nations.
1844	The opening up of the coffee trade with England gives Costa Rica the prosperity it had never had before.
1856	U.S. adventurer William Walker invades Costa Rica's Guanacoste region with several hundred mercenaries. Walker's forces are defeated at the battle of Rivas although Walker escapes. Drummer boy Juan Santamaria is killed in the battle and becomes one of Costa Rica's greatest national heroes.
1871-1925	The great era of the banana industry.
1921	Two-month border war with Panama ends after U.S. diplomatic intervention.
1948	Elections lead to a short civil war that brings Jose Figueras to power. A long period of peace and economic prosperity follows in the 60s and 70s.
1977	Sandanista rebels pursued into Costa Rican territory by troops of the Somoza regime in Nicaragua. Costa Rican police seal off the border.
1980s	U.S.-backed Contra rebels use Costa Rican territory to launch raids against the Sandanista government in Nicaragua.

1987 Costa Rican president Oscar Arias Sanchez, who had been elected in 1986, wins the Nobel Peace Prize for his efforts in developing a peace plan for the region.

1994 Tourist revenues exceed profits from banana exports for the first time in the nation's history.

1

The Rich Coast

Costa Rica, the smallest Central American country after El Salvador, covers an area of 19,653 square miles (50,100 square kilometers). First known as Nuevo Cartago (New Carthage) it was given the name of *Costa Rica* ("Rich Coast") by Christopher Columbus. Costa Rica is much longer than it is wide and it has a continuous volcanic mountain chain running the length of its territory. It is bordered to the north-west by Nicaragua, and to the south-east by Panama. It has two coastlines: in the west, the Pacific which extends for approximately 745 miles (1,020 kilometers), and in the east, the Caribbean, stretching for 130 miles (212 kilometers).

The Pan-American Highway runs down the west coast for 415 miles (662 kilometers). From east to west, between the ports of Puerto Limón, on the Atlantic, and Puntarenas, on the Pacific, there is a distance of only 188 miles (300 kilometers).

The country's population is estimated at 3.5 million spread out among the seven provinces of San José, Alajuela, Cartago, Heredía, Guanacaste Puntarenas and Limón.

One of Costa Rica's many beautiful beaches, lined with palm trees, on the Caribbean coast.

Costa Rica also has sovereignty over the island of Cocos which lies in the Pacific Ocean, 370 miles (600 kilometers) from Puntarenas. Cocos extends for only 9 square miles (24 square kilometers). It is believed to be the island where eighteenth-century pirates buried the treasure looted from Spanish galleons.

Of all Costa Rica's rivers, the San Juan (which flows along the Nicaraguan border and empties into the Caribbean), the mighty Rio Grande (which runs along the Panamanian border and flows into the Pacific), and the Reventazon are the most important. The smaller rivers—Abangares, Pirris and Savegre (which flow through the banana plantations of the lowlands), and the Diquis and its tributary the Rio Grande de Terraba (which reach the Pacific, north of the Osa Peninsula) also play their part.

Costa Rica has four volcanoes: Poas, 8,872 feet (2,704 meters), and Irazu, 11,586 feet (3,432 meters) are both active; Turrialba 10,955 feet (3,339 meters) and Barva 9,534 feet (2,906 meters) are extinct.

Although Costa Rica lies close to the Equator, its continuous mountain chain formed by the Cordillera de Guanacaste, Cordillera Central (containing the volcano Irazu) and Cordillera de Talamanca (running from north to south, with its highest peak Chirripo rising to 12,533 feet or 3,820 meters), keep it cooler than other more tropical countries. On the Atlantic side of the country are the plains which are hotter and steamier than the cool mountain areas which are often shrouded in mist. In the highlands, the maximum temperature is 75 degrees Fahrenheit (23 degrees Celsius). In the scorching hot coastal lowlands of the Pacific and Caribbean, with their extensive banana plantations, temperatures can rise to 95 degrees Fahrenheit (35 degrees Celsius).

Costa Rica has two seasons: the dry season, extending from December to May, and the rainy season from June to November. During the latter, the annual rainfall on the Caribbean coast can reach 77 inches (3,000 millimeters), and on occasions even more, and in the mountains and central valleys 30 inches (1,200 millimeters). The tremendous rainfall keeps the country lush and green so that Costa Rica is often called the "Garden of Central America." Trees and plants grow to immense proportions. In the

A view of Lake Botos, near Poas volcano, west of San José

cities, the rain sometimes causes flooding. But although the outlying suburbs of San José may sometimes look as if a deluge has hit them, the water soon drains away and the sun comes out again. During the rainy season the sun is shining at 6:00 a.m., but by noon the rains come. They last for much of the afternoon so that if you leave your home in the morning you need rubber boots and an umbrella for your return journey.

In addition to the effects of two active volcanoes, Costa Rica also suffers both earthquakes and less serious earth tremors. The old capital city, Cartago, was destroyed by two massive quakes, in 1841 and 1910. Usually the tremors are mild, often coming in a series of six, in rapid succession. Then inhabitants of the towns drop whatever they are doing and rush into the streets to find places of safety until the tremor has subsided.

As almost one-third of the country is covered by forests, Costa Rica has plentiful supplies of all kinds of exotic woods, such as mahogany, ebony, cedarwood and rosewood. The forests are more abundant in the *cordilleras* (mountain areas) and in the northerly province of Guanacaste. In that region, where *vaqueros*

An example of the lush, green, tropical vegetation that has earned Costa Rica its nickname of the "Garden of Central America."

(cowboys) drive their herds, grows the lovely deciduous tree called guanacaste which is known as Costa Rica's national tree. It is the perfect species for the hot plains as it gives plenty of shade both for the *vaqueros* and their herds.

Costa Rica's national flower is the hibiscus, but many kinds of flowers, all of them tropical and brilliantly colored, grow there. Orchids grow wild in wooded areas. In town gardens, butterflies of the brightest hues are drawn to the equally dazzling flowers of red, pink, yellow and blue.

As for animals, Costa Rica has all kinds of game in its forests. Huntsmen stalk red deer. Luckily, the government has restricted shooting to make sure the deer do not become extinct. In the jungle areas on the Panamanian border an amazing variety of creatures can be seen—from monkeys to crocodiles lurking in the muddy waters of the Rio Grande. Costa Rica has fifteen types of deadly snakes, such as the bushmaster and fer-de-lance which attack on sight, as well as many non-venomous ones. It is unique in having a species of toad (the *sapo*) which is highly dangerous, shooting poison at its victims from a range of up to nine feet (three meters). These deadly creatures lurk in pools and swamps, and frequently blind and kill domestic animals, as well as anything else that gets in their way. Spiders, lizards, cicadas, mosquitoes and other winged insects abound in the jungles. Brightly-feathered birds, such as parrots and *guacamayos* (macaws), fly from tree to tree squawking to each other. The jungle is never still. Steamy heat and intense humidity cause

A beautiful orchid growing wild in Costa Rica.

reptiles, insects, flowers and trees to grow much larger than they do in northern hemispheres.

On the *fincas* (farms), trees are laden with tropical fruit and coconuts. Local people like to slice off the top of a young, green coconut and drink the juice. Like the juice of the papaya, coconut juice is reputed to be good for stomach disorders. It is dangerous, however, to loiter under coconut trees. People have been knocked unconscious, even killed, by falling coconuts! Another source of danger is tap-water, especially outside San José. To avoid intestinal disorders all water must first be boiled.

In the markets of towns and country areas all kinds of exotic fruits and vegetables are sold, from mangoes, anonas (custard apples from the *guanabano* tree), guavas, bananas and papayas, to yams, maize and manioc (tapioca). Country-dwellers often set up their stalls on the highways to sell Central American fruits such as breadfruit, jak fruit and nance which are used domestically and rarely exported.

The people themselves, unlike those of most other Central American and South American countries, are predominantly Spanish. Less than two percent are Black (most of them live on the Caribbean coast) and about one percent are American Indian. Due to its stable government, other Europeans have settled in Costa Rica, especially Spaniards and Italians. There are also North Americans, who either work for American corporations or have retired to Costa Rica, and whom the Costa Ricans refer to as *gringos*.

One of the many types of colorful parrots to be found in Costa Rica.

A green iguana—one of Costa Rica's more unusual animals.

While the official language of the country is Spanish, English and German are heard in the chief cities, as well as some French and Italian. For this reason, Costa Rica appears more European than its neighbors. Ninety percent of the population is literate—the highest percentage in Latin America.

The state religion of Costa Rica is Roman Catholicism, but religious freedom is exercised. In addition to Catholics, there are Protestants, Methodists, Baptists and some North American sects, such as Quakers and Mormons.

Although Costa Rica is small, many countries (including Britain and the United States) have embassies there so that foreigners in Costa Rica can seek help and advice.

A palm tree, laden with fruit.

The Costa Rican flag which flies from public buildings is red, white and blue, and bears the national coat of arms.

Most visitors arrive in Costa Rica at Juan Santa María airport at El Coco, 10 miles (17 kilometers) by highway from San José. The national airlines, LACSA and Aero Costa Rica, fly to Costa Rica from main gateways in the United States, and neighboring countries. In addition, most major international airline companies have offices in San José.

Visitors coming by ship arrive either at the port of Puntarenas on the Pacific, or at Puerto Limón on the Atlantic coast. Both ports principally handle cargo but small numbers of passengers disembark there. However, many people choose to arrive by road, taking the excellent Pan-American Highway which runs from the Nicaraguan border, via Liberia in Guanacaste through San José to the Panamanian border. These days, travelling to, and in, Costa Rica presents no problems, but it was not always so easy and convenient.

2

Past and Present

Christopher Columbus discovered Costa Rica in September 1502, during his fourth and last voyage. He arrived at Puerto Limón during the rainy season. Although the country seemed to be sparsely populated, he called it Costa Rica—the Rich Coast—because the natives welcomed him with small pieces of gold. However, it was soon found that, far from being the rich country it had at first seemed, Costa Rica had no hidden treasures and no mountains of gold. So the Spanish armies which had ransacked neighboring Panama, Honduras and Colombia did not trouble themselves with Costa Rica. Since it had never known such civilizations as the Maya (an ancient tribe who had settled in Guatemala and Honduras), the Aztecs (of Mexico), or the Incas (of Peru), it had remained a poor and primitive country. Although the original inhabitants of Costa Rica had small quantities of gold from which they made golden objects, such as the *huacas* (artifacts made into the shapes of bats, frogs, eagles and tribal chiefs) of Panama, they did not make them on

Christopher Columbus, who discovered Costa Rica in 1502, during his fourth and last voyage to the Americas.

a grand scale, and few survived. But they did leave behind some remarkable pottery which can be seen today in the National Museum in San José.

The first Spanish settlers arrived in 1519. They noted that the central valleys were cooler than the coastal areas, and that gold could be panned in the rivers and later traded. It was also clear that the climate was suitable for the growing of crops such as maize. In those days Costa Rica came under the authority of the Captaincy-General of Guatemala. When the Spaniards arrived, they found Indians farming the land. But the Spaniards, landing in strange territory from another country, brought with them diseases previously unknown in Costa Rica. The Indians had no resistance against these illnesses, and many of them died.

It is thought there was little opposition to the Spaniards when they arrived in Costa Rica, unlike their bloody conquests in the rest of Central America. Gradually, the Indians and Spaniards settled down to work the land together. Unlike Honduras, Guatemala and Panama, there was little mixing of Indian and Spanish blood which is why, even today, the people of Costa Rica are mainly of Spanish stock and not mestizo (a mixture of Spanish and Indian).

In 1563, Juan Vasquez de Coronado founded Cartago and this was established as the capital of Costa Rica. For more than one hundred years the area around it hardly developed at all. It was not until 1717 that Heredía was founded, followed, as late as 1782, by the present capital San José.

Unlike the Spanish conquistadors in neighboring Central American countries (who got rich by trading the priceless treasures and rich gold stocks which they seized from the Indians), the settlers of Costa Rica were poor, having found only small supplies of gold. And they were obliged to exist as best they could, relying on the cultivation of crops.

Finally, in 1821, Costa Rica achieved its independence from Spain. For the next few years the country experienced a period of unrest during which Cartago ceased to be the chief city and San

José became Costa Rica's new capital. A stream of dictators ruled Costa Rica from 1835, when Braulio Carillo took command. In 1849 Juan Rafael Mora took over. He led Costa Rican troops against the American adventurer William Walker. Gradually, dictatorships gave way to democracy. Great changes took place. There was freedom of the press. Emphasis was placed on education and upheld by Mauro Fernandez, Minister of Education from 1885-1888.

The Indians continued to live in the hills of the north-eastern region of the country. The Spanish settlers, who by then were growing in numbers, began to fan out, starting up new settlements in Alajuela and elsewhere. They were still finding it hard to make a living from the land, and they began searching for new ways to grow rich.

In the early days they had noted that the cool valleys were ideal for the growing of crops. Now it occurred to them that not only would the fertile valleys be highly suitable for the production of coffee, but that if such a crop could be cultivated, it would bring in much needed revenue for Costa Rica.

Thus, in 1808, Costa Rica became the first Central American country to grow coffee. Today it is among the world's foremost coffee producers, exporting its rich, aromatic product all over the world. The coffee had been brought from Cuba. Very soon, the government was encouraging the peasant farmers to turn to coffee production, offering free land to anyone willing to work the crop. It did not take long for more and more small farmers to turn their hand to coffee-growing. Once they were able to get

A coffee plantation. Costa Rica is one of the world's leading coffee producers.

production started, they could earn more money than with any other crop, and could grow rich.

It was simple enough to grow the crop, but once the beans were harvested they had to be marketed and, in order to be traded, they had to reach a port. In those distant days, travelling by unpaved roads was slow and arduous. Mules were used to carry the coffee to the ports. By 1846, ox-carts had replaced the mules, trundling over the rough tracks to the port of Puntarenas. But those too were slow, and it was evident that if exports were to increase, faster transportation was needed. Today, the hand-painted, brightly colored ox-carts are a source of pride to Costa Ricans, and scaled-down models are often bought as souvenirs from city handicraft shops or from Fabricas de

Carretas at Sarchi (the factory that specializes in Costa Rican artifacts).

Four years later, in 1850, when more and more coffee was beginning to be sent to overseas markets, better transportation became a priority. A railroad was constructed to link San José with Cartago and Puerto Limón.

Observing that coffee production was the best source of income, more peasant laborers turned their attention to coffee growing. They created settlements along the River Reventazon, spreading out towards Turrialba. Any available land was quickly snapped up and turned into coffee-growing areas. The slopes of volcanoes were also used—and they proved ideal. Many farmers

An ox-cart laden with sacks of coffee. Before the railways were built, ox-carts were used to transport coffee from the plantations to the ports. Today they are a less familiar sight.

Loading containers with sacks of coffee. Improved transportation is an important factor in Costa Rica's increased export trade.

abandoned potato-growing altogether, opting for coffee which brought bigger rewards.

As the coffee plantations grew and expanded, transportation followed. From the central *meseta* (plateau) the population was spreading out like the tentacles of an octopus, by that time reaching as far as the Gulf of Nicoya in the Pacific.

While much of the Caribbean coast remained unpopulated, other areas of the country were expanding fast. Soon another new crop would improve Costa Rica's economy still further. That crop was bananas. Production began in 1878.

As in the case of coffee production, to get bananas to the ports so that they could be shipped all over the world, Costa Rica needed not only faster and better transportation but also a bigger labor force. The country's peasant farmers were already preoccupied with coffee-growing, so new labor was brought in from the West Indies. During the nineteenth century several thousand West Indians, many of them from Jamaica, were brought to Costa Rica to work in the banana plantations.

First, forests had to be cleared and the land prepared for the extensive banana plantations which were planned. As well as being the first Central American country to grow coffee, Costa Rica now became the first to grow bananas. By 1913, banana plantations stretched out along the Caribbean coast, providing millions of "hands" of bananas for export, and giving work to a new labor force.

It seemed as if Costa Rica was all set to grow rich with its coffee and banana trade when disease struck the banana plantations and drastically reduced exports. However, the big

Workers on a banana plantation near Limón.

banana companies, such as the United Fruit Company, which by that time were operating the plantations, turned the Caribbean coast over to the production of cacao and concentrated instead on the Pacific coast, where banana plantations soon became even more productive than the earlier ones of the Caribbean coastal plains.

These days, both the Pacific and Caribbean coasts are fully operational. The Caribbean plantations, having recovered, are producing more bananas than the plantations on the Pacific coast operated by the Standard Fruit Company. Banana plantations are big business for Costa Rica. The bananas they produce being among the largest and most delicious in the world.

Bananas are cut into "hands" before being washed and packed for export.

Today, cattle and abundant timber supplies help to boost Costa Rica's exports. The people have adapted to agricultural changes with the good humor for which Costa Ricans are noted. They cheerfully anticipate a stable future. Their country, which was ruled by Spain from 1530 to 1821, is today an independent republic.

3

The Stable Republic

Although Spain was no longer responsible for what went on in Costa Rica in the early nineteenth century, the country was still not completely in command of its own destiny. From 1824 to 1838 it formed part of the United Provinces of Central America. But Costa Rica still hankered after total independence, wanting to be self-governing and able to constitute its own laws without asking permission from the confederation. Eventually, due largely to Costa Rica's persistence, and the fact that the Central American countries which formed the confederation were so different from each other, the confederation was dissolved. This meant that at last Costa Rica was able to follow its own democratic principles. Today, the country is noted for its preservation of democracy and peace which marks it out strongly from such countries as El Salvador and Nicaragua, both of which have had turbulent political histories.

Costa Rica's constitution dates from 1871 but it has been amended on several occasions. A president is elected every four years, and government administration is carried out by the president and the thirteen ministers he has appointed. Government is democratic and consists of legislative and executive powers. The Legislative Assembly comprises sixty deputies who are elected for a four-year term. Executive power is exercised by the president, who is the head of the government. Voting is by ballot, and everyone aged eighteen years and over has the right to vote.

Although there are over a dozen political parties, the two main ones are the Liberal Party (*Partido Liberación Nacional*–PLN) and the National Unification Party (*Partido Coalición Unidad*). The PLN has dominated since 1949.

Costa Rica has been lucky to elect some popular presidents. One of the best-known was Dr. José Figueres (known as Don Pepe). He was president from 1953 to 1958, and again from 1970 to 1974. He did a great deal to establish Costa Rica's identity in Central America. Foreign ministers have always been conscious of representing Costa Rica in international affairs, and in particular at the United Nations.

As well as projecting a strong, democratic image to the world, Costa Rica also knows when to mind its own business. When in 1978/79 the government of Nicaragua's president, General Anastasio Somoza Garcia, was involved in a civil war in which there were an estimated 30,000 casualties, and *Sandinistas* (guerillas) gathered on Costa Rica's borders, there was a strong probability that Costa Rica might be drawn into the dispute. Wisely, Costa Rica stayed calm. The country had always shown a lead in diplomatic relations in Central America, and intended to continue to do so.

For this reason, Costa Rica differs greatly in a political sense from its Central American neighbors. It showed its intention to pursue and maintain a peaceful government by abolishing its army in 1949. It is also the only politically stable country in Latin America. But it does have a police force and a national guard, comprising over one thousand men, to maintain public order.

Even when the president attends public functions he has no elaborate motorcade of limousines, but simply an escort of

Members of Costa Rica's national guard which, together with the police force, maintains public order.

A young schoolgirl in San José. Costa Rica has the highest literacy rate of any country in Latin America.

motorcycles. It is hardly surprising that Costa Rica is known as *el pais de la amistad*–"the country of friendship."

Democracy is not the only thing that sets Costa Rica apart from the rest of Central America. Its educational system is enlightened and progressive. With the highest literacy rate in Latin America, its educational program serves as a model for its immediate neighbors. Primary and secondary education in Costa Rica is both compulsory and free. So too is pre-school education. There are so many schools, both public and private, that a very

37

wide choice exists, ranging from schools which adopt the United States teaching system, known as American schools, to German gymnasiums and French lycees. (Lincoln College in the San José suburb of Moravia is an example where pupils wear neat uniforms and study from American textbooks.)

Costa Rica has two universities, the University of San José which has various departments including architecture and engineering, and the National University at Heredía which has marine and veterinary science departments as well as traditional faculties.

On account of Costa Rica's political stability, its good educational standards and its great desire to maintain peace, many Europeans and Americans have settled there, building homes on the coast or settling in the towns. The affluent suburb of San Pedro in the capital, San José, has as its residents coffee estate-owners, diplomats and foreign businessmen who often commute between Costa Rica and Europe and the United States. In a politically stable country their businesses can flourish. They also assist the Costa Rican economy by their technical expertise.

Some have left Europe and the United States to live in a country which rates peace as a priority. These days, there are in Costa Rica many retired European and North American businessmen who count themselves fortunate to live in a country which has a long history of political calm.

Those accustomed to the political upheavals of Latin American countries might find Costa Rica a shade too peaceful

Fishermen landing their catch at Puntarenas in the Gulf of Nicoya.

at times. But *pensionados* (pensioners—those who have retired), *rentistas* (financiers) and the North American businessmen (who have settled in Costa Rica attracted by the low cost of living and who can spend their time fishing in the Gulf of Nicoya or flying their private planes down to Jaoo beach) would not think so. Most expatriates settle down, perfectly content to make the most of their leisure time in a climate which, although not always perfect due to the high rainfall, is sunny and warm most of the time.

Like other Latin American countries, Costa Rica has its share of official public holidays. During Holy Week which covers the Easter period from Maundy Thursday to Easter Monday, businesses close and the people celebrate, first by going to Mass and then by holding street fiestas and carnivals. May 1st is Labor Day. Corpus Christi is celebrated in June, and Guanacaste Day in July. In August, comes the Feast of the Virgin of Los Angeles, followed by Independence Day celebrations in September, and then Columbus Day in October—a big event for much of Latin America.

Costa Ricans take time off for Christmas and the New Year. As these two festivals fall during Costa Rica's dry season, many people like to celebrate on the beaches with barbecues and lots of cheerful music. Costa Ricans especially love the *salsa* and *marimba*—two well-known dance rhythms—and they never miss an opportunity to get to their feet whenever they hear them.

Along the beaches and in cafés of port cities, such as Puerto Limón and Puntarenas, the blare of trumpets competes with the ocean surf as Costa Ricans leave their tables to give spontaneous dance performances. Their natural rhythm and grace often make the occasion as professional as any theater dance troupe. Many of the rhythms and dances originate in Cuba but that does not prevent the Costa Ricans from claiming them as their own. Also popular is the *cumbia* from Colombia. These days some of the entertainers and artists who record Latin American rhythms originate in Costa Rica. Much in demand are Spanish recording stars and British and American rock groups.

The streets of Puntarenas and Limón resound with the *salsa* as only native artists can play it, with the sure touch that comes from growing up listening to that unmistakable beat. In the streets of San José recordings of the *salsa* echo from music shops

The National Theater in San José.

and arcades—the youth of Costa Rica are almost as crazy about native rhythms as about those imported from America. San José has a fine National Theater (*Teatro Nacional*) where native and foreign dance troupes, and international musicians and actors perform.

Fast achieving recognition are some of Costa Rica's "primitive" artists who paint scenes from the life around them in bright, bold colors—from street-markets with traders carrying baskets of exotic fruits to picturesque scenes of coasts and mountains. Though not as advanced as some Latin American countries (such as Colombia, Venezuela, Mexico and Panama which specialize in the plastic arts), Costa Rica, nonetheless, is developing its own style.

  Artists, writers and musicians, in particular, need a sympathetic atmosphere in which to produce their best work. Costa Rica, the most stable Central American country, provides that kind of environment for all its inhabitants, whether they are Costa Ricans or people from other lands.

4

Living in Costa Rica

The first thing you notice about Costa Rica, in comparison with its neighbors in the rest of Central America, is its peaceful, orderly atmosphere, and the lack of hustle and bustle. Even in San José, traffic flows at a regular pace and there is little of the "overtake at any cost" attitude found in other Latin American cities. However, despite the lack of blaring horns, trucks are noisy, belching out diesel fumes from their exhausts and polluting the atmosphere.

Costa Rica has 22,121 miles (35,600 kilometers) of paved roads which include almost 3,000 miles (4,830 kilometers) of highway, incorporating 405 miles (653 kilometers) of the InterAmerican Highway which links San José with other provincial cities. The Pan-American Highway traverses the country from Panama to the Nicaraguan border. From San José to Panama, the Pan-American Highway passes through the old capital of Cartago. From San José to the Nicaraguan border it continues past El Coco airport to Heredía and Alajuela. On some stretches the road is a dual highway and, as it is completely

A narrow road in the Highlands.

paved, travel through the country is fast and easy, with much of the highway passing through spectacular scenery.

International buses use the Pan-American Highway, leaving San José and journeying to Penas Blancas on the Nicaraguan frontier. There are also buses to Managua, the capital of Nicaragua, and to Panama City. Tourists can take excursions both to the interior and to the coastal regions, and to Costa Rica's renowned beauty spots, such as the Orosi valley with its beautiful rolling landscape, Sarchi, the Irazu volcano, and the former capital Cartago. Buses also leave from San José and Alajuela for the Poas volcano. In the cities, there are plenty of taxis and the rates charged are reasonable.

SANSA, the national domestic airline, operates internal flights from San José's Juan Santa María airport to Liberia (Guanacaste province), Limón, Golfito, Tamarindo and Puerto Quepos.

Juan Santamaría International Airport is 17 kilometers outside San José and is the main international airport. The national Costa Rican airlines are LACSA and Aero Costa Rica. They fly from the United States to Costa Rica and other Central American countries.

Costa Rica has 590 miles (950 kilometers) of railroad. A large portion of the railroads are plantation lines used by the banana companies. Most railways are state-owned, and lately, have suffered from lack of funding and neglect. Most have been replaced by roads. National railroad lines link San Jose with Puntarenas and Limón.

For those who like traveling by train, the journey from San José to Puerto Limón is a spectacular trip. Although the distance is only 103 miles (166 kilometers), due to the terrain, the journey takes eight hours with the train making more than fifty stops en route. Leaving the station at San José in the morning, the train travels along the Reventazon valley to Turrialba and Siquirres where it makes a stop before continuing. Along the narrow-gauge track which winds through the jungle, travelers may catch a glimpse of a monkey, a parrot or a macaw. Many people like to travel at the rear, standing on the platform and observing every aspect of the jungle as the train moves slowly along the track. At each stop vendors crowd aboard to sell food, drinks and fruits, from *gallitos* (small tortillas), to corn, beer and jak fruit.

Once the train leaves Siquirres, it travels through the lowlands towards Limón along a narrow track which was constructed in 1870. The 100-mile (160-kilometer) track took twenty years to build. Such were the terrible conditions in the jungle that six thousand workers died of malaria and yellow fever. Of all the workers, the Jamaicans were the only ones who could withstand the appalling tropical diseases. Many settled in the area and their families remain to this day with their homes close to the railway.

The track from Siquirres to Limón is only 25 miles (40 kilometers) but the train travels slowly, jerking precariously from side to side so that the journey seems much longer. On this stretch the land is flat, with cacao and banana plantations spread out on either side. For the last 10 miles (16 kilometers) the railway follows the coastline, running alongside giant coconut palms. Finally, the passengers disembark at the steamy port of Limón where there is always a crowd to greet them, for a trip on the jungle train is a big adventure. On the return journey the passengers can fly back to San José, take a bus, or stay with the train, if they are not in a hurry.

In each of the cities a good network of buses traverses the center and the suburbs. Often they are filled with commuters, schoolchildren and students on their way back and forth to offices, schools and colleges. Costa Ricans get to their offices early to start their day at eight o'clock in the morning when the sun is already shining brightly. Government offices open from 8:00 a.m. to 4:00 p.m., Monday to Friday. Commercial offices operate from 8:00 to 11:30 a.m. and from 1:30 to 5:30 p.m.

Banks are open from 9:00 a.m. to 3:00 p.m.; shops from 8:00 a.m. to 12 noon and from 2:00 to 6:00 p.m. Some shops close on Saturday afternoons. Costa Rica has handicraft centers in the larger towns where ceramics, objects made from wood, and leather goods can be found. There are also plenty of street-markets where coffee, fruit, vegetables, household articles and handicrafts can be bought.

Costa Rica has an automatic telephone system in San José and other provincial capitals, such as Limón. International telex and telegram facilities are available at San José, Limón and Puntarenas.

Costa Rica has two Industrial Free Zones—at Puerto Limón

Craftsmen at work in Sarchi. There are handicraft centers throughout Costa Rica where ceramics, wooden and leather goods are made.

The National Bank and other bank buildings in San José—an example of modern Costa Rica's economic growth.

and Puntarenas—for the development of the manufacture of food, domestic appliances and clothing.

Banking facilities in the country are good, with some banks operating into the late afternoon. There are four main commercial banks which were nationalized more than thirty years ago. These include the Banco Nacional de Costa Rica with eighty-one branches, the Bank of America, the Banco Anglo Costarricense with seventeen branches and the Banco de Costa Rica with twenty branches. There are other smaller banks too. A strong black market exists in U.S. dollars, operated, among others, by street dealers who loiter outside international hotels to do business with foreigners.

While the capital San José has modern hotels, provincial capitals and the port cities of Puntarenas and Limón offer hotels of a more traditional type, designed on a more modest scale.

The country has three national newspapers: two daily ones, *La Nacion* and *La Republica* and one evening newspaper *La Prensa Libre*. The *Tico Times* is an English-language newspaper published weekly in San José and is of particular interest to North Americans living in Costa Rica.

There are five commercial television stations, one of which transmits directly from the United States via satellite. They transmit local interest programs, national news, feature films, serials and educational programs.

Cinemas in the towns show American films with Spanish subtitles, but few are the latest Hollywood productions. Even in San José they are dated by comparison with those movies showing in London, Paris and New York. Other films on view are Spanish or Latin American with an occasional dubbed French or Italian film.

Medical care is good in Costa Rica. As well as private clinics, there are free Social Security hospitals, such as the Juan de Dios in San José, so everyone can receive medical treatment whatever their financial status.

Most Costa Ricans enjoy a reasonable standard of living, considerably higher than most of Central America. Most of them are actively employed in the ports, on the land and in the cities. Their homes range from the smart, colonial-style houses of the fashionable suburbs, such as San Pedro in San José, to the more modest one-story houses in the provincial towns and outlying areas. Almost all of these homes display bright, tropical flowers and shrubs in their front gardens.

In the port cities of Limón and Puntarenas the less well-off Costa Ricans make out as best they can, living in clapboard houses close to the harbors or banana plantations. In such humidity they need few clothes and tend to dress casually as do most Costa Ricans, even in the cities, where the only people in business suits are usually foreigners. Costa Ricans prefer to discard the necktie and formal clothes in favor of the more comfortable short-sleeved shirt and jeans.

Most Costa Rican cities are laid out on the block system with *avenidas* (avenues) and *calles* (streets), having numbers instead of names, and *plazas* (squares).

Tropical flowers and shrubs in a typical Costa Rican garden.

A typical tree-lined street, with a background of modern office blocks. Even the businessmen buying their morning newspapers are dressed casually on account of the heat.

Costa Rica has no food specialties of its own, except *gallo pinto* ("speckled hen")—a dish of rice and beans which is frequently eaten at breakfast by the poorer families as well as at lunch and dinner. Maize pancakes and *platanos* (plantains) form their staple diet. Costa Ricans like snacks; and they often eat *tortas* (pastry envelopes filled with meat), *empanadas* (pies) and *tortillas* (omelettes).

Following the trend towards fast food, young Costa Ricans

frequent hamburger bars and Pops shops, famous in Costa Rica for their American-style ice-creams. Horchata, a drink made from rice flour is popular but not as popular as other American soft drinks. Crema de Nance, a yellow-colored sweetish liqueur made from the fruit of the nance tree which grows in Costa Rica, can be sampled in some city bars and restaurants though it is now getting more difficult to find.

The Atlantic and Pacific beaches enable Costa Ricans to fish, (sea fishing is excellent in Costa Rica), swim, sail and spend their leisure time by the ocean. Puntarenas is a superb fishing area for marlin and tarpon, attracting many Americans from the Florida coast. Most of the large hotels also have swimming pools. One favorite resort is Oja de Agua—a spa which is a short drive from San José. In addition, both San José and Puerto Limón have golf courses.

Guanacaste province provides good hunting for deer. It is good riding country too. Among other sports, soccer, the national sport, is very popular in Costa Rica, with matches taking place at San José's National stadium. In 1984, Rugby Union was established with the formation of the San José Rugby Union Association. The British and French living in Costa Rica had been playing the game for some time and, when they realized the Costa Ricans were interested, it was not long before they set about founding a club.

Costa Rica also has National Parks full of wildlife and tropical vegetation where armadillos, monkeys, raccoons, snakes, turtles and wild pigs, as well as hundreds of birds and butterflies, can be

Palm trees silhouetted against the skyline at sunset in Tortuguero National Park. The park also includes a Caribbean rainforest.

seen. While cock-fighting is permitted in neighboring Panama, it is illegal in Costa Rica, although in some country areas fights are staged and the organizers hope they will not run foul of the law.

But, like other nations, as well as filling in their leisure time, Costa Ricans also have to work. Costa Rica today offers many job opportunities from agriculture to land development and the buying, selling and renting of property.

5

Earning a Living

As the country is mainly agricultural, over half the population earns its living by farming. Costa Rica relies heavily on its coffee, bananas, beef, sugar and cocoa exports. As a result, many Costa Ricans work in the plantations and in cattle-raising, but others find a living in a variety of different occupations.

As almost one third of the country is forested, many species of woods are found which are used to produce timber (so far timber production in Costa Rica is operated only on a small scale) and for house construction, furniture and wooden artifacts. (Throughout Costa Rica lovely mahogany and ebony objects are sold in craft shops.) Costa Rica also grows orchids and other exotic flowers, both wild and cultivated, which are exported.

Because of the high level of annual rainfall and the fertility of the soil, Costa Rica has been able to cultivate a wide variety of staple crops including maize, beans, sweet potatoes, yams, *manioc* (tapioca) and potatoes. In poorer homes *platanos* (plantains) are frequently substituted for potatoes at mealtimes. Costa Ricans also prefer rice to maize and sometimes serve it for breakfast. Cattle-breeding also is gaining importance in Costa Rica with much of the beef going to the United States.

By contrast, although Costa Rica has over 750 miles (1,200 kilometers) of coast on the Pacific and Atlantic, commercial fishing has not been developed on a large scale. The Costa Rican government continues extending its fishing limits so it can export on a productive scale.

Minerals are not sufficient so far to add much to the export budget. Unlike some of its neighbors which, at the time of the Spanish conquest, were rich in gold, Costa Rica had much less than the amounts found in Panama or Honduras. Today gold and silver-production is still minimal. However, substantial quantities of sea salt are produced, and deposits of sulphur and manganese have been discovered. It is debatable whether or not they will prove sufficient to work economically. So far, sulphur deposits amount to very much less than iron ore deposits. But these, and bauxite, could be developed to increase Costa Rica's economy.

Hydroelectric power is a growing source of energy in Costa Rica. The Arenal hydroelectric plant was opened in Guanacaste in 1979. Hydroelectric power has the potential to supply domestic needs with enough surplus for export. An oil refinery operates at Puerto Limón. The government is interested in developing its oil industry and encourages oil companies to bid for offshore concessions.

Cultivated land near San José. Ten percent of the land in Costa Rica is used to grow crops and a large portion of the population earns its living by farming.

In the general industrial sector, food-processing, chemical production, and plastics are steadily expanding. A petro-chemical plant, and the expansion of the fishing industry by the construction of a processing plant at Golfito (the banana port in the south of Costa Rica, close to the Panamanian border) are two projects that contribute to the port's handling of one-fifth of Costa Rica's seaborne trade.

Agriculture remains as the chief source of productivity, with

10.4 percent of the land used for crops, such as sugarcane, potatoes, beans and maize. Thirty-one percent of the land is forested, and forty-six percent is used for pastureland. While production in the coffee and banana plantations has remained high, labor relations have worsened and some strikes have ensued as a result of increases in the cost of living. When the National Liberal Party came to power in 1982, headed by Luis Alberto Monge, it introduced tough economic measures to stem inflation and stabilize the economy. In 1996 the main exports were coffee, bananas, textiles, consumer goods and raw materials.

Most of Costa Rica's exports go to the United States, Germany, Nicaragua, Britain, and Canada. Its imports come

Fertile fields where cattle graze. Dairy cattle are playing an increasingly important role in Costa Rica's agriculture.

Young sugarcane. Sugar is an important crop in Costa Rica.

from the United States, Japan, Venezuela, Mexico, Guatemala, El Salvador, Panama, Germany and Britain.

Costa Rica's chief competitors in the export markets are the United States, Japan, West Germany and the Central American Common Market. After the imposition of economic measures which restricted imports, first in 1980 and again in 1982, Costa Rica approached the International Monetary Fund (IMF) to determine if a loan could be raised to assist the country's ailing economy. By no means the poorest Central American country, Costa Rica had suffered a blow when commodity prices fell. The Nicaraguan civil war of 1978-9 hampered trade dealings still further. Today, manufacturing industry is slowly beginning to improve with light industry and agriculture continuing to top the list in Costa Rica's export markets. There are plans to improve the heavy industries by the construction of a cement plant and a fertilizer plant.

Costa Rica is a member of the Central American Common Market as well as having free trade agreements with Nicaragua, Panama and El Salvador. In order to develop its economy, Costa Rica is obliged to seek monetary aid from overseas banks.

Aid has been offered to enable Costa Rica to develop its agriculture, to improve the water supply of San José and to set up an animal husbandry school where students could take three year study courses. Money has also been provided for forestry work and the development of crafts.

With aid from banks, and loans from other international sources, Costa Rica can begin gradually to make improvements in the economy and in the standard of living of its population. Costa Ricans are hard workers: they want to see their country prosper. Although Costa Rica is not rich and the wages earned by laborers are low, the standard of living in the country is high when compared with the rest of Central America. Wherever Costa Ricans work and whatever their wages, they can receive free medical attention in hospitals and clinics, and free education for their children. The social welfare system provides them and their dependents with work-injury, sickness, maternity and disability benefits.

Life in Costa Rica is not as difficult as in the rest of Central

America where housing is both expensive and difficult to obtain. Transportation in Costa Rica is adequate, the attitude of the people is closer to Europe than Latin America, and there are no long afternoon siestas to delay business negotiations.

European-style market gardening has also set Costa Rica apart from its neighbors. The volcanic soil of the *meseta central* (central plateau) has proved ideal for coffee-growing. The "arabica" type of coffee (literally Arabic) grown in the central valleys has earned a reputation for being one of the best coffees in the world. Sugarcane, cotton, cocoa and tobacco all boost Costa Rica's

A coffee bush.

exports. Total coffee production is over 142,600 metric tons a year.

Standard Fruit Company employs a large portion of the labor force on its banana plantations. Working on the plantations is a different way of life from that of the towns. City-dwellers find their employment in banks, the hotel industry, manufacturing, insurance, real estate and other commercial enterprises.

6

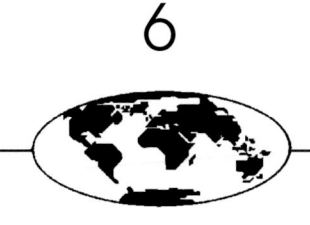

San José: The Quiet Capital

San José, lying almost in the center of the country, in a valley of coffee plantations, at an altitude of 3,773 feet (1,150 meters), became Costa Rica's official capital in 1823. With a population of 330,000, it has an equable climate ranging between 58 degrees Fahrenheit (15 degrees Celsius) and 78 degrees Fahrenheit (26 degrees Celsius). Costa Ricans call themselves *Ticos;* the people of San José are called *Josefinos.*

The city is laid out on the grid (geometric system) with *avenidas* (avenues) running from east to west, and *calles* (streets) running north to south. The main city thoroughfares are the Avenida Central (Central Avenue), Avenida 2 (Second Avenue), and the Calle Central (Central Street) which are usually clogged with traffic. Smaller streets lead off the main intersections. These are full of shops, bars, restaurants, offices and other commercial ventures. Away from the central areas which run into *plazas* (squares), the streets consist of neat, clapboard houses, painted in a variety of colors. On the outskirts they are surrounded by picket fences and their gardens are usually bright with flowers. Although San José's buildings often give it a shantytown appearance, they are built in contemporary Latin American fashion. There are no skyscrapers or tower blocks. The only building of real distinction is the National Theater.

Parks and small squares add to San José's quiet atmosphere. It is rare to hear raised voices, except in the municipal market where tropical fruits, vegetables and Costa Rican handicrafts can be purchased.

The National Theater is one of Costa Rica's most prized buildings. It lies off the Avenida Central on Calle 3, opposite the colonial-style Gran Hotel de Costa Rica. Built in 1897, the theater is frequently praised for its superb architecture. The people of San José are especially proud of their theater. Inside there are sweeping marble staircases, and a foyer decorated with Venetian mirrors, chandeliers, frescoes and sculptures by Pietro Bulgarelli. There are also statues of Beethoven and the Spanish writer Calderon de la Barca. Ballet companies, dance ensembles, international musicians and theater groups perform there.

The Legislative Assembly of Costa Rica meets in the Palacio Nacional (National Palace). Any member of the public is at liberty to attend debates.

San José's best-known buildings are the National Museum which houses a fine collection of pre-Columbian artifacts, the Biblioteca Nacional (National Library), a large imposing building with a vast collection of books in all languages, the Union Club (open to members only) where Costa Ricans like to

A view of San José, Costa Rica's capital city.

read newspapers and catch up on the city's news, the Gold Museum (Museo de Oro) in the Banco Central (Central Bank), the metropolitan cathedral, and the immense General Post Office (Correos y Telegrafos) built in 1916.

The Gold Museum, though small by comparison with Colombia's Museo de Oro in Bogota, is, nevertheless, a treasure-house of Costa Rica's gold ornaments made by the American Indian tribes of the country who were at work long before the Spanish conquest. The gold objects depict chiefs, gods, eagles, bats and frogs. There are nose ornaments, breastplates, and a variety of other elaborate decorations.

The Post Office building, a short walk away, is usually bursting with Costa Ricans and foreign visitors. While they mail parcels, airmail letters and send telegrams, it acts as an ideal meeting-place where items of news can be exchanged.

Masses held in the metropolitan cathedral on Avenida 2 are attended by many Costa Ricans. A building of simple grandeur, it contains religious paintings and sculptures. It is the most imposing of San José's many churches, but there are other interesting ones, such as the Iglesia la Merced and the Iglesia la Soledad in the Bellavista district.

San José has its share of medical centers, such as the Dr. Caldera Guardia Clinic and the San Juan de Dios Hospital, where residents of the city can receive free medical attention. Costa Rica also has a Red Cross Society (Cruz Roja Costarricense).

Avenida 2, one of the main streets in San José.

One of the main churches in San José. Most Costa Ricans are Roman Catholics.

Close by Avenida 9 is the penitentiary. The Fabrica Nacional de Licores (the Liquor Factory) is situated beside the Parque Espana. Long before you reach the factory you can smell the sickly odor of molasses, for rum is made there, as well as Crema de Nance (a liqueur made from the Costa Rican fruit called nance). Opposite the Parque Espana is the Casa Amarillo (Yellow House), home of the State Department of Costa Rica.

Like other Central American cities, San José has several parks where residents can stroll and pass the time of day. Right in the heart of the city, at the junction of Avenida 2 and the Calle Central, lies the Parque Central (Central Park) facing the cathedral. Although small, the park contains many tropical trees. City residents come to Central Park to sit and read their newspapers, to hold lively conversations, and to have their shoes cleaned and polished by the *limpias botas* (boot-blacks) who are often small boys interested in earning a few *colones*.

The Parque Morazan in the Otoya district has a stone statue of Simon Bolivar, the liberator of five Latin American countries. In the Parque Nacional (National Park) there is a bronze monument (by the French sculptor Rodin) to the five Central American countries which rid themselves of the American adventurer William Walker who, in 1860, with his band of men,

A street vendor in San José.

A peaceful scene in one of San José's parks.

captured New Granada, as Central America was then called.

    The Parque Bolivar houses San José's zoo, where sloths, tigers, monkeys, bears, jaguars and much of Costa Rica's wildlife can be observed. The zoo is well laid out, enabling everyone to get a good view of the animals among the tropical vegetation. San José also has a snake laboratory where some of the country's snakes are kept and their serum extracted for medical use and research. Some of the most deadly snakes live there.

    The Paseo Colon runs west heading towards the sports complex of La Sabana, the home of the National Stadium. La Sabana also has a race-course and gymnasium. Costa Ricans make use of all the sporting amenities available. Their Country Club (open to members only) offers facilities for a variety of sports. There is an Olympic-sized swimming-pool and there are clay courts for tennis—a sport fast gaining in popularity in Costa Rica.

San José's residents live in a variety of houses, ranging from the extensive colonial-style homes found in the wealthier suburbs to the less expensive clapboard houses. On the whole they favor rambling single-story properties where they have space to move and tend their gardens.

El Pueblo, a large commercial complex developed by a Colombian architect, is a short distance from the city center. Constructed in traditional Latin American style, the boutiques, restaurants, craft-shops, discotheques and bars have proved extremely popular. In El Pueblo can be found Mexican restaurants and those serving Costa Rican dishes, shops selling a variety of handicrafts, wine-cellars and coffee-shops.

Hotels in San José vary from the traditional Gran Hotel de Costa Rica in the heart of town to the modern deluxe Hotel Irazu on the outskirts; and from the Cariari (the most expensive) 4 miles (7 kilometers) from the city, near the Juan Santa María airport, to the cheaper, self-catering Apartotels. Restaurants offer a range of food from French cuisine at *Le Mirage* and *La Bastille* to Cuban and local dishes.

San José has embassies and consulates, cinemas, museums with exhibits of jade, pre-Columbian jewelry, modern paintings and sculptures, and bookshops which sell foreign language editions as well as Spanish books. The Mercado Nacional de Artesania is the place to find genuine local handicrafts, many of them made from all kinds of woods.

Posters advertise a variety of entertainments from concerts to craft exhibitions. Life in San José is lived at a leisurely pace with none of the frenetic dash and pace of much larger Latin American cities. Buses trundle up and down the main thoroughfares disgorging their passengers. Fares are cheap, so Costa Ricans can ride around without great expense. At weekends, they escape from the city by getting into their cars, or boarding buses and journeying into the countryside. But they always come back to their capital. Visitors, too, feel immediately at home in San José on account of its friendly atmosphere.

Fourteen miles (twenty-two kilometers) east of San José lies the former capital, Cartago. Earthquakes have damaged the city on a number of occasions, the last in 1910. Its 120,000 inhabitants admit that they fear another earthquake might occur soon. And, looking at the volcano Irazu, they often wonder about volcanic eruptions too. Irazu erupted in 1823, 1910 and 1963. After the last eruption, ash was blown as far as Puntarenas, a distance of 70 miles (112 kilometers).

Cartago's fine eighteenth-century basilica of Nuestra Señora de Los Angeles (Our Lady of the Angels), the patroness of Costa Rica, attracts scores of pilgrims who attribute healing powers to *La Negrita* (the Black Virgin). On August 2nd (a *fiesta* in Cartago), the Virgin's statue is carried in procession through the streets and great celebrations take place, with band music and dancing in the square. The old parish church of Cartago

Looking towards Cartago, Costa Rica's former capital.

suffered badly in several earthquakes and was almost completely destroyed in 1910. Today, its ruins form part of the Botanical Gardens where visitors can sit and count the *picaflores* (hummingbirds) and butterflies.

From Cartago it is a twenty-mile (thirty-kilometer) drive to Turrialba, situated in a rich coffee-growing region. The town itself is undistinguished with rows of rickety shops and cafés. But the countryside around it is beautiful with many small villages situated in the mountains. Turrialba volcano reaches 11,000 feet (3,700 meters).

West of San José an *autopista* (highway) joins the Pan-American

Highway leading to El Coco. Further on, the city of Heredía is soon visible. Heredía, 6 miles (10 kilometers) from the capital, has been dubbed "the city of flowers." It is the chief city of the province of Heredía—an area of coffee plantations and cattle-raising, which was settled by Spaniards from Andalusia. Adobe houses with red tiled roofs, and with gardens filled with flowers, give Heredía a distinctly colonial air. Costa Rica's National University is located in the city.

Continuing a further 8 miles (13 kilometers) along the Pan-American highway the traveller reaches Alajuela—an old town and capital of the province of the same name. Alajuela, with its Saturday market, is a popular weekend resort for residents of San José. It is also an important coffee, sugar, fruit and livestock center. On the outskirts of the town is the well-known bathing spa of Oja de Agua. From Alajuela many make

The huge, smoking crater of the Poas volcano.

the journey to the Poas National Park where the still-smoking Poas volcano with its crater, over 4,920 feet (1,500 meters) wide and 1,000 feet (330 meters) deep, can be seen.

From Alajuela the road passes through the town of Sarchi, where replicas of the traditionally painted ox-carts and cowhide rocking-chairs can be bought; and on towards Grecia (a pineapple-growing area) and San Ramon, until it reaches Puntarenas.

7

The Port Cities: Puntarenas and Puerto Limón

Puntarenas, once one of Costa Rica's major ports on the Pacific Ocean, is built on a peninsula which juts out into the Gulf of Nicoya. A distance of 68 miles (109 kilometers) from San José by road and 73 miles (116 kilometers) by rail (a four-hour journey), Puntarenas has a population of 35,000. Many of its inhabitants are Blacks who work in the banana plantations.

Puntarenas has a hot, humid climate with a mean temperature of 86 degrees Fahrenheit (27 degrees Celsius). The city itself is typical of a port with dockyards, wharves and casual laborers looking for work. As the region produces bananas, cotton, pineapples, coconuts and rice, the lifestyle centers around the plantations and dock areas. Once a thriving port, these days Puntarenas has a rundown look. Houses are simple clapboard— often shabby and ramshackle. They line the road into the port, surrounded by lush, tropical vegetation. In the sticky heat the residents loll outside drinking juice from coconuts. They wear as little as possible to try to keep cool, but usually pull on straw hats to deflect the sun which can be intensely hot, especially at midday. Even when the days are cloudy it is possible to suffer severe sunburn. Children play in the gardens of their dilapidated homes and usually a few scrawny hens are scratching around.

Some of the hotels in Puntarenas that are set in a tropical location right on the gulf once attracted fishermen from the United States. But, since the economic recession, the hotel business has floundered in many areas and some proprietors have had to sell at considerably reduced prices.

The port of Caldera is now handling most of the cargo on the Pacific coast. Puntarenas is a shadow of its former self in the days when it shipped huge stocks of bananas across the world, and when the illicit drug trade flourished. Hotels reflect its shoddy, down-trodden appearance. Instead of traditional restaurant/cafés, cheaper Chinese restaurants now fill the town.

Yet for all that, deep-sea fishing in Puntarenas remains among the best in the world, and fishermen hire boats and tackle, or bring their own to fish the Gulf of Nicoya for marlin. From Puntarenas boats sail to the islands in the gulf, known as Islas Negritos. There is also a ferry service to Playa Naranjo. Many people prefer to swim at Jaco beach, south of Puntarenas, which has better bathing and modern hotels. The beach at Puntarenas used to be muddy and not too clean but is presently looking much more appealing.

San Lucas island can also be reached by boat from Puntarenas. It has a penitentiary of an unusual kind—the inmates can study,

The Gulf of Nicoya, a favorite spot for deep-sea fishing.

work (earning a small wage), have visitors to stay, and enjoy a privacy unknown in most countries' jails.

Costa Rica's possession, called Isla del Cocos (Cocos Island), is uninhabited. It is now a wooded national park which can be reached by air or boat, providing permission for the visit has been obtained from the Costa Rican government. Cocos Island, once thought to be the hideout of pirates and the location of their buried treasure, offers good fishing and underwater swimming, but attracts few visitors. Those who venture there are usually biologists, researchers or those curious to see if they can find buried treasure beneath the coconut palms. The weather on Cocos Island can be unpredictable and visitors can easily be caught in an unexpected cloudburst.

On the mainland, Puerto Quepos in Puntarenas province was constructed as a banana-exporting port by United Brands. Once a favorite haunt of Costa Rica's middle classes, Puerto Quepos, like the port of Puntarenas, is now run down. The beach is still in good shape, although nowhere near as fine as the beaches of Manuel Antonio, east of Quepos.

At Monteverde, a high altitude forest forms part of a National Park supported by the World Wildlife Fund. Many species of birds, reptiles and monkeys can be seen here alongside exotic trees, giant ferns and orchids. The weather is generally cool, especially after rain.

Puerto Limón is the only deep-water port on the Atlantic coast. It is Costa Rica's most important harbor—the place where Christopher Columbus first set foot on Costa Rican soil. Once

San Lucas island in the Gulf of Nicoya, the site of a penitentiary where prisoners are allowed to work or study.

A view of the primary cloud forest at Monteverde.

an ancient Indian village called Cariari, Limón is more African in atmosphere than Central American, especially during its Salsa Festival when the whole town comes out to celebrate, and strident Afro rhythms hit the streets. Most of Puerto Limón's inhabitants are Blacks and it is they who give the town its exotic air. Open-air cafés and bars are alive with talk in the humid atmosphere.

Puerto Limón has a population of about 57,000 and is the largest town on Costa Rica's Caribbean coast. Its *mestizo* population (of mixed Spanish and American Indian descent) makes it very different from other Costa Rican towns. Limón's inhabitants have a great liking for Caribbean music and dancing. They are friendly, lively people who like to dance and make merry.

The town is laid out in a geometric pattern with a few new

hotels on the fringes. Most, however, are of the traditional type. Limón's palm trees, with their white-painted bases, give it a genuine Caribbean touch.

Limón is principally a fishing and banana port. New docks have been added, and offshore oil speculators are drilling for oil. People come to the port just to see the bananas being loaded, for Puerto Limón handles over two million "hands" of bananas annually.

Bus services in Limón are erratic. When buses eventually arrive they are often packed to capacity, so many residents take to motorcycles or cycles, or simply walk. Puerto Limón's airport is situated three miles (five kilometers) from the center. SANSA, the domestic airline, operates daily flights to and from San José. Flying time is about twenty minutes. Puerto Limón has a Social

Paper being loaded for export in the port of Limón. Costa Rica's extensive forests provide a ready source of raw materials.

Security hospital opened in 1982 and a Protestant church.

North of Limón lies Moin which has docks suitable for container ships and tankers, as well as a reasonable beach. Boats set sail from there for Tortuguero—an area which has become famous as the preservation site for Costa Rica's green turtles. Turtles lay their eggs at night during the months of July to September. Tortuguero is a National Park, part of which contains a Caribbean rain forest. In Tortuguero, visitors can get an idea of the jungle by taking a boat through the waterways. Here it is possible to spot armadillos, sloths, monkeys, otters, crocodiles and hosts of birds, such as kingfishers, toucans and egrets, and

An egret walking the beach in Costa Rica.

One of the many brilliantly colored butterflies which are found in Costa Rica.

also brilliantly-colored butterflies. But there are also plenty of mosquitoes, ticks and *coloradillas*—fleas which burrow into the skin, called chiggers. Like the Atlantic railway, known as the "jungle train," which runs from San José to Limón, the Tortuguero trip is a great adventure.

Not far distant, at Valle de Estrella, there are extensive banana plantations owned by the Standard Fruit Company. Further south, the road leads to Cahuita whose narrow strip of beach forms a conservation area of the Cahuita National Park, containing a coral reef, white and black sand, and the wreck of a Spanish ship. Scuba divers and snorkellers are much attracted by the area.

At the foot of the Talamanca range lies an Indian reserve—which seems close to the Panamanian border and the hot, steamy

Tall mangrove trees in the Corcovado National Park. These tropical trees grow in swampy areas.

jungles. At Palmar Sur—a banana plantation area 61 miles (98 kilometers) from the Panama frontier—pre-Columbian stone spheres, thought to be used for the study of astronomy, can be seen. Once you reach Palmar Sur you get the sensation you have already arrived in Panama. The heat prickles with intensity and there is a general air of lethargy. Rio Claro, less than a mile (two kilometers) away, has two hotels where travellers can escape the heat by taking a dip in the pool before crossing the border. As the road approaches the frontier, the surface gets bumpier. At Paso Canoas the shops are filled with luxury goods from Panama. Costa Ricans can buy consumer items, such as domestic appliances, much more cheaply than elsewhere in their own country. Fashions here are more stylish too.

Inland from Limón lie the Rio Frio (Cold River) banana plantations and the towns of Guapiles and Siquirres. At the most southerly end of the country lies Golfito, a town separated by a distance of over 1.5 miles (2.5 kilometers) from its banana port.

The Osa Peninsula is reached by boat from Golfito. At the western end of the peninsula lies the Corcovado National Park which includes the Isla del Caño. Here there are swamps and tropical rain forests just as nature intended them. The rain forests are the home of snakes, insects and wild pigs. Chiggers infest the swamps and pastures, particularly up country in Guanacaste, Costa Rica's north westerly province.

8

Guanacaste: Cowboy Country

It is immediately noticeable that Guanacaste is different from the other six provinces of Costa Rica. It has a character and style all of its own. Guanacaste is cattle country; the land of the *vaquero,* the Texas of Central America, the area which contrasts strongly with the *meseta central* and the humid coastal plains. The people, many of them *mestizos,* cling to their folklore traditions.

The province of Guanacaste is an agricultural region with a population of 228,250. Liberia—its chief town and capital—is the home of 40,000 people. It is a partly forested area, with exotic trees and flowers. Yet, at its lower, southerly end—the peninsula of Nicoya—it consists of an area of beaches bordering the Pacific. In the highlands are found all kinds of game—from jaguar to peccary and tapir.

The rolling land is dotted with small farms where farmers produce crops of maize, rice, beans, cotton and many kinds of tropical fruits, as well as raising herds of cattle. Around Liberia

A Zebu bull, a breed highly resistant to tropical diseases, on a farm in the Nicoya peninsula.

lie the big cattle ranches from which *vaqueros* (sometimes called *savaneros*) drive their herds across the *llanos* (lowlands), looking as if they have strayed out of the Wild West. They wear boots, tough trousers (often with leather leggings), checked shirts and wide-brimmed hats to keep off the sun and rain. It rains hard in Guanacaste during the wet season, turning the prairies to mud. The cowboys have to be experts at handling both horses and cattle in all kinds of weather conditions.

In the dry season, dust flies as the cowboys round up their herds. The cattle are fat and sleek in the Costa Rican lowlands, usually ending up as intended meat for the export markets.

The inhabitants of Guanacaste eat well. In addition to good beef, fruits and vegetables, they have an abundance of fish both in the rivers and in the Gulf of Nicoya. Wood from the forests provides them with timber for house construction.

They are friendly and hospitable people who welcome strangers to their *haciendas* (ranches) where hunting trophies often adorn the walls. Many do not see the need to make more than the occasional visit to their capital—a distance of 134 miles (216 kilometers). But, if they do visit Liberia, the wealthy ranchers often fly there in their own private planes. They have learned to be self-sufficient, organizing their estates as they see fit. The cattlemen also enjoy a tough but free and easy life, riding for most of the day, from sun-up to sundown, driving the cattle herds

Tourists riding through the rainforest.

across the plains. It is a life they would not exchange for the motor traffic and city ways of San José.

After dark, the people of Guanacaste love to enjoy music and dancing. Once the *vaqueros* have slipped out of the saddle they are ready to enjoy themselves. Guanacaste has its own official national dance—the *punto Guanacaste*—just as it has its own tree, the guanacaste. Musicians improvise with an assortment of instruments. The trumpet and guitar are most popular. It is rare to see a flute, unlike in the music of the Andes regions in neighboring South America. The rhythms of Guanacaste are usually those of the marimba, heard throughout Costa Rica, but there are always variations on popular themes.

The music shops of San José sell recordings of the music of Guanacaste. It sounds softer and more gentle than the strident rhythms of the *salsa*. Its distinctive sound is reminiscent of the wide open spaces, of horses and cattle ranches, and of the *savaneros* who make the prairies their home.

Liberia, the capital of Guanacaste, is a typical cattle town with neat rustic houses and a modern church which looks quite out of place. The people of Liberia have grown accustomed to seeing strangers in town; it is easy for them to spot foreigners in cattle-raising territory. Buses bring visitors to Liberia from various parts of Guanacaste and elsewhere, but there are few hotels and, if it can be arranged, it is much preferable for visitors to stay at an *hacienda* where they can sample the real life of the rancher.

Liberia, with its backdrop of the Cordillera de Guanacaste, is a town in which few visitors linger, for on the way to the Nicaraguan border lies Santa Rosa with its National Park incorporating the last entire dry tropical forest in Costa Rica. (The vegetation of a dry forest varies greatly from that of a rain forest.) Many botanists and biologists go to Santa Rosa to study the flora. One hour's drive from Liberia, Santa Rosa offers the chance to see tropical vegetation and wildlife in its unspoiled state. At Santa Rosa, animals such as armadillos, deer and herons can be observed at close range. There, in the dry tropical forest, it is even possible to see monkeys, bats and coatimundis.

The beach areas of Guanacaste are hot, and the mosquitoes ferocious. There are also sandflies which can be thorough pests. Although turtles lay their eggs on the beaches, these are not often seen since coyotes are notorious for getting there before anyone else and making a meal of the eggs. Fortunately, turtles lay eggs in sufficiently large quantities to ensure that at least some survive.

Guanacaste province also has a 49,420-acre (20,000-hectare) National Park called Rincon de La Vieja, which conserves the area around the volcano of the same name, and includes part of a dry tropical forest and some hot sulphur springs. For anyone who wants to get the real feel of the country, National Parks offer a glimpse into tropical vegetation and wildlife at close quarters.

On the peninsula of Nicoya, which forms part of Guanacaste province, is the Barra Honda National Park. This park was set up to protect caves which had been discovered in the area and

A turtle on a Guanacaste beach

were considered of interest. Although there are remains of a dry tropical forest at Barra Honda, it is the caves that warrant attention. Some are too difficult for the amateur to penetrate, but Terciopelo Cave can be viewed, with its fine stalagmites and stalactites. The *cascadas* (cataracts flowing over limestone cliffs) are also of interest. It is best to visit Barra Honda in the dry season; during the rainy period the area is muddied and wildlife scattered.

The Palo Verde National Park is an area of marshes where ornithologists can study waterfowl. The Nicoya peninsula, jutting into the Pacific Ocean, has some good beach areas as well as conservation areas and these are easy to reach from the town of Nicoya. The town claims to possess one of Costa Rica's oldest churches. Buses run from here to Liberia and to San José, but few roads are in good repair and trucks are the best form of transport over such bumpy terrain. However, the Nicoya peninsula gives the visitor the feeling of having left the beaten track, and the fine scenery and often deserted beaches compensate for the rough ride.

One of the most popular areas, not only with inhabitants of Guanacaste province but also with Costa Ricans from San José, is Papagayo Bay and its beach Playa del Coco. Once the islet with its rugged headland was a peaceful paradise. But these days Playa del Coco is often overcrowded. It can seem particularly brash after the tranquility of the capital, and the wide open spaces of the prairies.

However, Playa del Coco is not the only beach of the peninsula. There are many others, including Playa Hermosa, Playa de Panama and Playa Junquillal. They can all be reached by bus from Liberia. At weekends, the inhabitants of the towns wait at the bus stations to pile into the noisy, air-polluting vehicles with their foul-smelling exhaust fumes which will transport them to the ocean and back again. For Costa Ricans the ocean is the great escape. They seem not to mind the tedious journey in overcrowded and overheated buses. Once they reach the beach, they like to keep active by playing football or tossing frisbees to each other. Often they hire boats to drift out on the swell and survey the beach crowds from a safe distance.

Samara, 29 miles (47 kilometers) from Nicoya, has the safest bathing, and many families go there for weekends and vacations.

Like all popular beaches, Samara has its crowds and its litter. But, for a while at least, having a good time is all that matters to the Costa Rican weekenders. They cannot wait to shake off the dust of the city and dive into the ocean.

Guanacaste province, with its 295-feet (900-meter) high mountains, savannas (lowlands) and coastal areas, is a province of many contrasts and many differing aspects of nature. The people of Guanacaste are open-hearted, welcoming the stranger and making him feel at home.

9

Costa Rica in the World Today

With a stable government and a policy of peace, Costa Rica should be the land of opportunities, but so far it has not been assertive in imprinting itself on the world map. Though not cut off from the rest of Central America—indeed it is very aware of what is going on—Costa Rica seems content to mind its own business and get on with its own affairs. It is that very attitude which appeals to many of its newer residents, such as the colony of retired North Americans who have built or bought homes in the country and are there to stay.

A policy of peace and a continuation of political stability is admirable, particularly so in troubled Central America, but it could be that Costa Rica is being just a little too complacent about the future. In many ways it has a right to be pleased with itself. It has made the greatest social advances of any of the Central American countries, and its political system is democratic. It has the highest standard of living in Central America, and the fastest-growing population. Its inhabitants are mostly of Spanish descent, which means that in some respects they are closer to Europe than to Central America. They have a good health program where everyone, rich or poor, can receive medical aid. Their educational system is the envy of Latin America. And yet, something seems to be missing. What is it? Could it be that unpredictable restlessness which characterizes the rest of Latin America? Do the Costa Ricans take themselves a little too seriously, preferring to cling to old traditions rather than look towards a future which might bring about changes in their country?

The visitor finds no slums on the scale of those in Venezuela, Colombia or Mexico. He finds only the ramshackle dwellings in the port cities to indicate that, like other Central American countries, Costa Rica also has its poorer relations. But they are not very evident. There are no hordes of beggars to be seen, though sadly they are increasing, because more country-dwellers are drifting into cities like San José to find work and often they end up homeless and without jobs.

The Costa Rican ports may look shabby and rundown but the inhabitants are neither desperate nor destitute. Germans, Italians and North Americans have settled in Costa Rica, setting up new businesses or branches of their business empires based in cities as far afield as Milan, Hamburg, Chicago and Miami. Others are executives in North American companies or are employed by multi-national conglomerates. They find Costa Rica a much more peaceful and friendly place in which to work than downtown New York and other big U.S. cities.

Unlike many parts of Latin America, in Costa Rica's cities there are few kidnappings, murders or serious crimes. There are some muggings however, and Costa Rica is not without its jails. The only thefts one is likely to encounter are small-time operations such as stealing from cars, or pickpocketing on the streets.

In Costa Rica you can sleep easily in your bed and not be scared of burglars or prowlers. But too much tranquility makes for monotony and many young Costa Ricans leave the country for American cities such as Miami, New York and Los Angeles, finding more opportunities there to stretch their talents. As they leave, so the North Americans move in. They are generally businessmen, or *pensionados* (retired pensioners) who are glad to slow down and slip into the role of senior citizens, after a lifetime of decision-making.

In Costa Rica there is no rush and tumble. Everything gets done without a scramble. Transportation, though it could be better, is adequate. In addition to the few unpaved country roads, the Pan-American Highway makes towns easily accessible.

LACSA and Aero Costa Rica, the international airlines, serve a wide network of foreign cities. SANSA and Travelair, the domestic lines, take care of Costa Rica's chief towns by making regular daily flights.

Most Costa Ricans are accustomed to dressing in a casual way. Although they are not seen wearing Bermuda shorts on the avenues of San José, they are not dressed in formal business suits either. Jeans and casual shirts are the standard dress for the young, both male and female. Not so long ago, fashions in Costa Rica tended to be dreary with none of the trends found in the Caribbean and the rest of Latin America. These days, clothes are arriving in Costa Rica's boutiques and department stores (still small and conservative) from Florida, California, Guatemala and Panama. The hand-printed shirts of Costa Rica, many of them adapting the traditional designs found on the *carretas* (ox-carts) can be bought in the shops, as well as the *guayaberas* (short-sleeved embroidered cotton jackets) found throughout Latin America. Leather goods, although not of the finest quality, are also popular in Costa Rica. Many articles, such as belts and wallets made of crocodile and python skin, can be found in the shops of San José alongside hand-tooled leather bags. Model ox-carts, mahogany artifacts—from bunches of grapes to bangles, salad bowls and egg cups—are all on sale, as are hand-painted trays and gold-plated reproductions of *huacas*, once fashioned in solid gold by the now extinct Indian tribes.

Costa Ricans are becoming more conscious of current trends, not only in fashion but also in food. Hamburgers and ice-cream appeal to the young considerably more than tacos and gallo pinto.

Costa Ricans have a democratic government and everyone over the age of eighteen has a right to vote. Although, from time to time, they may complain about politicians—some presidents have been more popular and forward-looking than others— they appreciate the fact that no president so far has involved them in

A hand-painted, brightly colored ox-cart. Scaled-down models of carts such as this are popular souvenirs.

the political upheavals experienced by the rest of Central America. Throughout the Civil War and political unrest in Nicaragua, El Salvador and Cuba, Costa Rica has remained calm, advocating a policy of peace not war. No other Central American country can claim to have enjoyed so many years of political stability.

Costa Rica can offer a great deal in terms of stability and peace. Since developing countries need loans and grants from international agencies, such as the World Bank and European Development Fund, there are plenty of opportunities for foreigners to invest in Costa Rica. Two *Zonas Francas* (Industrial Free Zones) in Puerto Limón and Puntarenas, devised for the development of industry, make it even easier to do business. The Free Zones are adjacent to the ports. There is good transportation both by road and railway, and equipment and machinery for imports and exports are exempt from tax. Trade exhibitions and Fairs to encourage business of all kinds are growing.

Because of the uncertain political situation in Central America, trade in the Central American Common Market—of which Costa Rica is a member—has suffered. But, once the political situation rights itself, this is expected to improve.

The port of Caldera in the province of Puntarenas is taking over much of the work once handled by the port of Puntarenas, while Puerto Limón remains as Costa Rica's chief port.

The banana plantations of the Atlantic coast have made their comeback (after being wiped out by disease) and are now Costa Rica's most productive. Labor relations in the plantations have not always been good in recent years, but the strikes are now over and full production has once again been established.

Though not financially among the richest nations in Latin America, Costa Ricans are wealthy in other, more important aspects. They have a social security service, good hospitals, free education and, above all, a reliable, democratic government. They live in a country where their voices can be heard, yet there is no sign of political rallies, no heated debate on street corners, no banner waving. Costa Rica has not earned its title—"the Switzerland of Central America"—for its green pastures alone but also for its political situation. The only elements likely to erupt in Costa Rica are the three still-active volcanoes—Poas, Arenal and Irazu.

Christopher Columbus believed Costa Rica must be full of gold and that is why he called it "the rich coast." He was just as surprised when Costa Rica proved to have no valuable treasure as visitors are today to discover that, far from being just another volatile banana republic, Costa Rica has its own unique identity..

Shedding its army in 1949, it proclaimed to the world its policy of peace. Even General Somoza, the then president of Nicaragua (engaged in a Civil War with the Frente Sandinista de Liberacion Nacional in 1978/9) could do nothing to involve Costa Rica in war-torn Nicaragua. Costa Rica bravely made a stand for peace, and it continues to do so. Costa Rica is a peaceful country, and the Ticos, as the Costa Ricans are called, intend to keep it that way.

El Pais de la Amistad—"the country of friendship." That is Costa Rica. It is a country where *con mucho gusto* ("with pleasure") is heard more often than any other phrase.

GLOSSARY

bauxite	Ore from which aluminum is made.
carretas	Ox-carts.
colones	Costa Rican currency.
conquistadores	Spanish soldiers.
cordilleras	Mountain areas.
fincas	Farms.
gringos	Costa Rican term for North Americans.
haciendas	Ranches.
huacas	Artifacts made in various shapes such as bats, frogs, eagles and tribal chiefs formed with solid gold by the ancient Indian tribes.
hydroelectric power	Electricity generated by water power.
maize	Indian corn.
marimba	Latin American dance rhythm.
mestizos	People with a racial mix of Black and Indian.
plantains	Large banana-like fruit grown in most Latin American countries that must be cooked before being eaten.

salsa	Well-known Costa Rican dance.
savannas	Lowlands.
Spanish galleons	Large heavy sailing ships used for war and commerce by the Spanish between the 15th and early 18th centuries.
Ticos	Costa Ricans.
vaqueros	Cowboys.

INDEX

A
Aero Costa Rica, 22, 45, 94
agriculture, 26-33, 54, 56-57
airports, 22, 45, 94
Alajuela, 7, 13, 72
American Indians, 20, 24, 26-27, 64, 78, 81, 95
architecture, colonial, 49, 57, 69
art, modern, 41-42, 63, 65, 69
art, pre-Columbian, 24-25, 63-64, 69
Atlantic coast, 15, 22, 77

B
bananas, 8, 11, 12, 30-32, 97
banking, banks, 47-48
beaches, 52, 77, 88, 90-91
birds, 18, 52, 71, 77, 80
Blacks, 20, 50, 74, 78
Bolívar, Simón, 10
buses, 44, 46, 70, 79, 87, 90

C
cacao, 32, 46, 54
Caribbean coast, 15, 20, 30-32, 78
Caribbean Sea, 7, 13
Carillo, Bravlio, 27
Cartago, 10, 13, 16, 26, 29, 70-71
cathedrals, 64, 65
cattle, 18, 33, 54, 55, 72, 84-87
Cavallon, Juan de, 9
Central American Common Market, 59, 97
churches, 65, 70, 80, 87, 90
climate, 15, 16, 39, 62, 76-78
coconuts, 19, 74, 76
Cocos Island, 14, 76
coffee, 8, 10, 11, 27-30, 60-61
Colombia, 40, 42
Columbus, Christopher, 9, 13, 24, 77, 98
Confederation of Central America, 34
conquistadors, 9
Coronado, Juan Vasquez de, 9, 10, 26
cost of living, 39, 57

D
dances, dancing, 40-41
Desamparados, 7
Diquis, 9
disease, 10, 46
Don Pepe (Dr. José Figueres), 11, 35

Drake, Sir Francis, 10
dress, 50, 82, 94-95

E
earthquakes, 16, 70-75
education, 37-38, 97
El Salvador, 13, 34, 58-59, 96
English language, 21, 49
Europe, Europeans, 20-21, 38, 58, 60, 96
exports, 8, 28-33, 57-58, 77, 85

F
festivals, 39-40
Figueres, Dr. José (Don Pepe), 11, 35
fish, fishing, 8, 52, 55, 76, 79, 86
flag, 22
food, 51-52
foreign aid, 96, 97
forest areas, 17, 18, 31, 80, 84, 86, 88, 89
fruit, 19-20

G
gold, 24-25
Gonzalez, Gil, 9
government, 8, 34-37, 95-96
Guanacaste, 11, 13, 17, 84-91
Guatemala, 24-26, 95

H
haciendas (ranches), 86
handicrafts, 47, 69-70, 95
health, 19, 49, 59, 65, 68, 80, 97
Heredía, 10, 13, 26, 72
Honduras, 24, 26
housing, 49-50, 69

hydroelectric power, 55

I
imports, 57-58
independence, 26, 33
industry, 47, 56, 59, 96-97

J
jungle, 18-19, 45-46, 80-82

L
LACSA (airline), 45, 94
language, 8
Liberal Party, 35, 57
Liberia, 23, 45, 84, 87, 90
Limón, 7, 45-46
literacy rate, 8, 21

M
markets, 19-20
meseta central (central plateau), 30, 60
mestizos, 78, 84
minerals, 55
Monge, Luis Alberto, 57
Mora, Juan Rafael, 27
mountains, 7, 13, 15
museums, 25, 63-64
music, 40, 87

N
national parks, 52, 67, 77, 88
National Theater, 41, 63
National Unification Party, 35
Nelson, Horatio, 10
newspapers, 49, 64, 67
Nicaragua, 7, 13, 34, 35, 43, 57, 59, 96, 98

Nicoya, Gulf of, 30, 39, 75, 89-90
Nicuesa, Diego de, 9

O
oil, 55, 79
Osa Peninsula, 15, 83

P
Pacific coast, 13, 15, 22, 32, 52, 56, 75
Pacific Ocean, 7, 13-15, 30, 74, 84
Panama, 7, 11, 13, 14, 23, 24, 26, 42, 43, 44, 58, 59, 82, 95
Pan-American Highway, 13, 23, 43
parks, 63, 66, 67
pirates, 10, 14
police force, 36
politics, 34-38, 95-96
population, 7, 13, 24
public holidays, 39-40
Puerto Limón, 13, 22, 24, 29, 77-80
Puntarenas, 13, 22, 45, 74-77, 97

R
railways, 29, 45
rainfall, 15-16, 39, 54, 89
recreation, 49, 52, 66-69, 76, 90-91
religion, 8, 21
Reventazon River, 7, 14, 29
Rio Grande, 7, 14, 18
rivers, 14-15, 18, 25, 29
roads, 43, 71, 73, 90, 94, 97
Roman Catholicism (*see* religion)

S
salsa, 40, 78, 87
Sanchez, Oscar Arias, 12

San Isidor de El General, 7
San José, 7, 9, 10, 13, 26, 29, 45, 62-70
San Juan River, 7, 14
SANSA (airline), 44, 94
Santamaria, Juan, 11
schools, 37-38
Spain, Spaniards, 20, 24-27, 34, 63-64, 81, 93
Spanish language, 21, 49, 69
Standard Fruit Company, 32-61, 81
standard of living, 49-50, 59, 93, 97

T
telecommunications, 47
television, 49
timber, 17, 54
Tortuguero National Park, 80-81
tourism, 8, 12
transportation, 22-23, 30, 45-46, 94
Travelair, 94
Turrialba, 15, 29, 71
turtles, 80, 88, 89

U
United Fruit Company, 32
United Provinces of Central America, 11, 34
United States, 11, 21, 22, 38, 39, 49, 52, 55, 57, 75, 93-95
universities, 38, 72

V
vaqueros (cowboys), 17-18, 84-85
vegetation, 18, 52, 68, 77, 84, 88
volcanoes, 15, 16, 29, 44, 70, 71, 88, 98

103

W
Walker, William, 11, 27, 67
West Indians, West Indies, 31
wildlife, 17-19, 45, 52, 68, 77, 80, 84, 88, 89